WHY I LOVE ERNEST

Laurel Richardson

South Street Press
Worthington, Ohio

WHY I LOVE ERNEST
South Street Press
Worthington, OH

Copyright: 2018 by Laurel Richardson (text) &
                Ernest Lockridge (artwork)
All rights reserved

ISBN-13:978-1986062756

ISBN-10:1986062759

Cover Design: Ernest+Mr. R.

www.laurelrichardson.9@gmail.com
www.ernesthugh@gmail.com

WHY I LOVE ERNEST

A Baker's Dozen of Reasons

Presented to

Ernest Lockridge

On the Occasion of

His Seventieth Birthday

Revised on the occasion of

His Eightieth

Laurel Richardson

SEDONA PETROGLYPHS

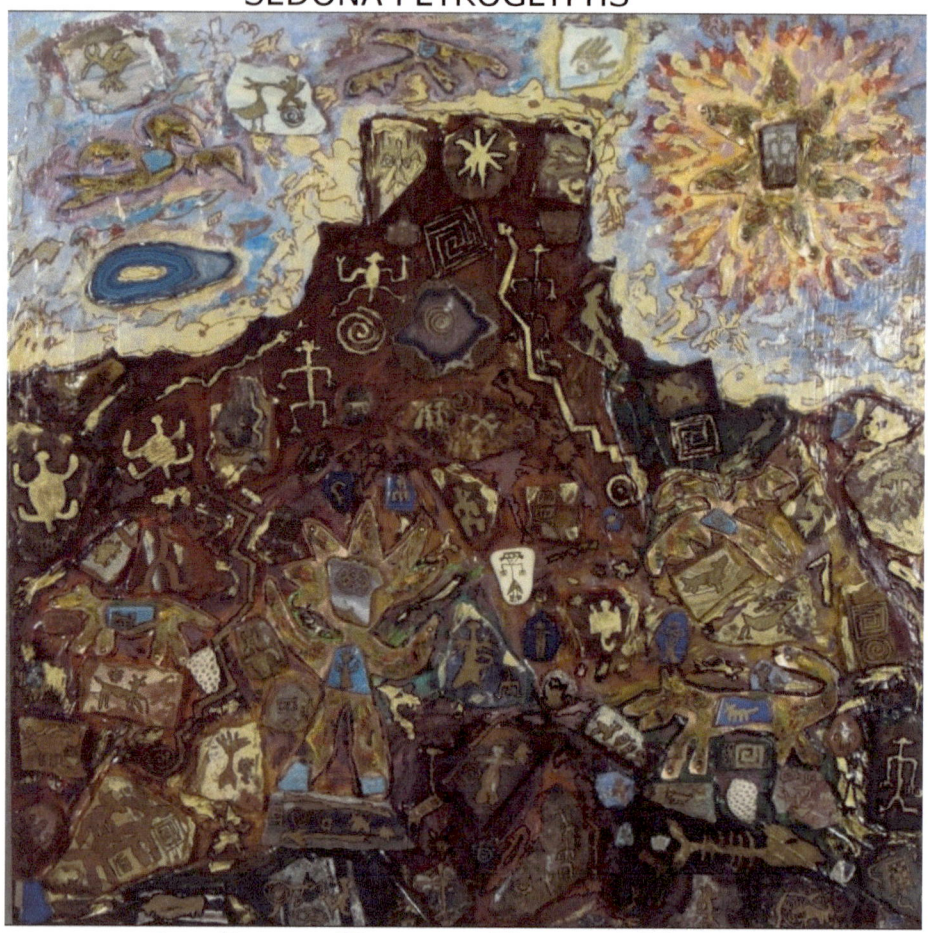

Acrylics on Stone on Plywood 23x27

INTRODUCTORY

In 2008, when Ernest's seventieth birthday was approaching, I wanted to do something special to mark the occasion, to celebrate why I love him. I surreptitiously took photos of him and his paintings and wrote vignettes about his life as an artist. These vignettes were probably the only writings I did not ask him to edit. I wanted to surprise him.

I brought the collection of photos and vignettes to OFFICE MAX for a Specialist to make them into a book, which he did, a spiral-bound one.

Spiral binding is not my favorite but, when I presented it to Ernest on his birthday, he cried.

He said it was the nicest present he had ever received.

I love the guy.

****

At the start of 2018, I suggested to Ernest that he make a book with photos of his paintings as gifts for our friends, children, and grandchildren. He demurred.

A month later he came to me with a book mock-up based on the spiral-bound book I had given him ten years earlier. He had changed out some of the paintings ("Those older ones are so primitive."), corrected my grammatical hiccups, and had prepared it for CreateSpace so it could be published with a genuine spine!

He was too modest to publish a book of his art but willing to share with me the creation of this book, revised and expanded, in honor of his eightieth.

Of course, I love my guy.

WHITE NIGHTS, ICELAND

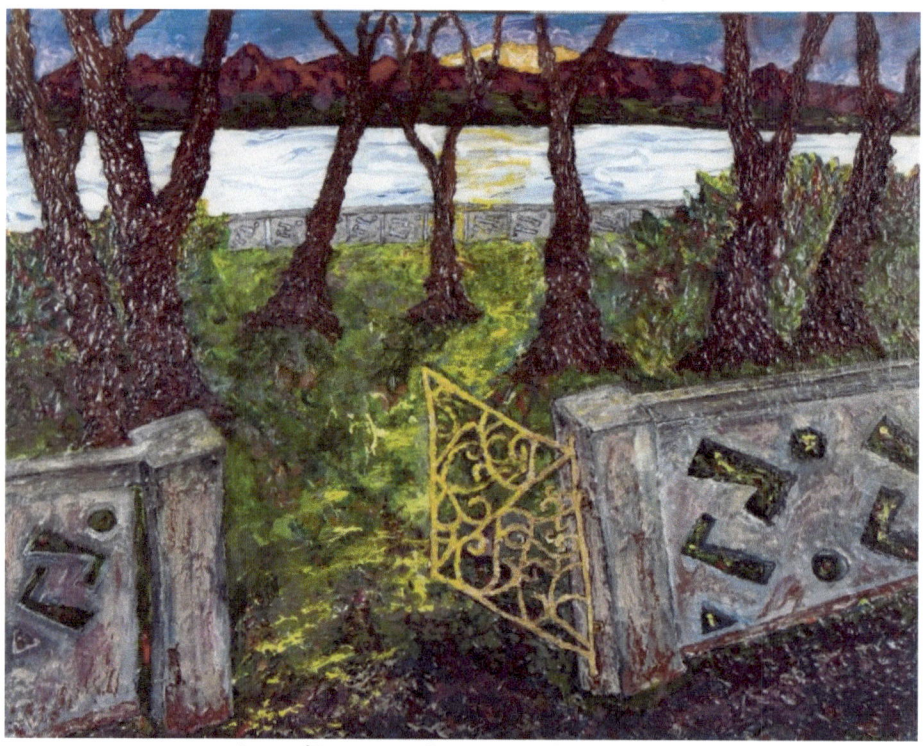

Acrylics on Canvas 24x36

REASON ONE

Ernest is in the back yard; he has a gessoed canvas balanced on two horses. To his left is his mother's old folding table, overflowing with makeshift cardboard boxes of Sobo and Golden Acrylics, plastic tubs, and brushes. To his right is the All-Purpose Ladder, draped with paint-splattered cloths. He's wearing a tattered and stained "Genuine Red Dirt" Sedona t-shirt, tattered shorts, and worn-out Tevas. A little yellow-tipped Walkman antenna rises above his head.

Less than a month ago, when I was visiting my BFF Betty in the hospital, he decided to give me a cheer-up homecoming surprise. Knowing how much I love Rothko's paintings he said he would paint me one. But Ernest being Ernest he painted four of them, each 20x30. Then he thought he'd try some paintings inspired by Jackson Pollock. He painted three of those. And now he is painting in his own style, lettering "ERNEST" in red in the lower right hand corner. Van Gogh, he tells me (as if I didn't know) signed his name "VINCENT."

Ernest's paintings—there are thirteen of them now—are bright and vivid, richly undertoned, and overlaid with colors he creates in the bottom of plastic tubs. His brush never collects the same color-mixture twice.

The interior walls of our house had reflected my gentle water-color sensibility; now they blaze with Ernest's deep golden yellows and orangey red acrylics, alive with splatter from unused house paints I had rejected as being too bright, and awash in Van Goghish landscapes and architectural images.

In his paintings outside and inside—nature and culture—reflect into one another; that which humans have created exists along with, melds with that which is a given—land, sky, sun, plants. He loves painting outsized thickened leaves.

I like watching him, as I am now, painting quick, certain strokes, lathering it on, walking away, looking at his work, walking around it, returning, doing a dos-a-do dance with the canvas.

Although I have repeatedly repainted my living room I have never liked being in it. Over the years, I have hired feng shui experts to help me figure out why; their "cures," such as red-tasseled mirrors and cascading crystals, never worked—aesthetically, or any other way. But with forty feet of the "Rothko" triptych on one wall, Bermuda on another, Sedona over the fireplace, I spend a lot of time in the living room, stretched out on the couch, piles of magazines on the floor at my fingertips. Mimi, our yellow cat, is in there, too.

We have expropriated Ernest's customary after-dinner spot, and he hasn't said a word.

WHERE THE SUN CROSSES THE NORTHERN SKY

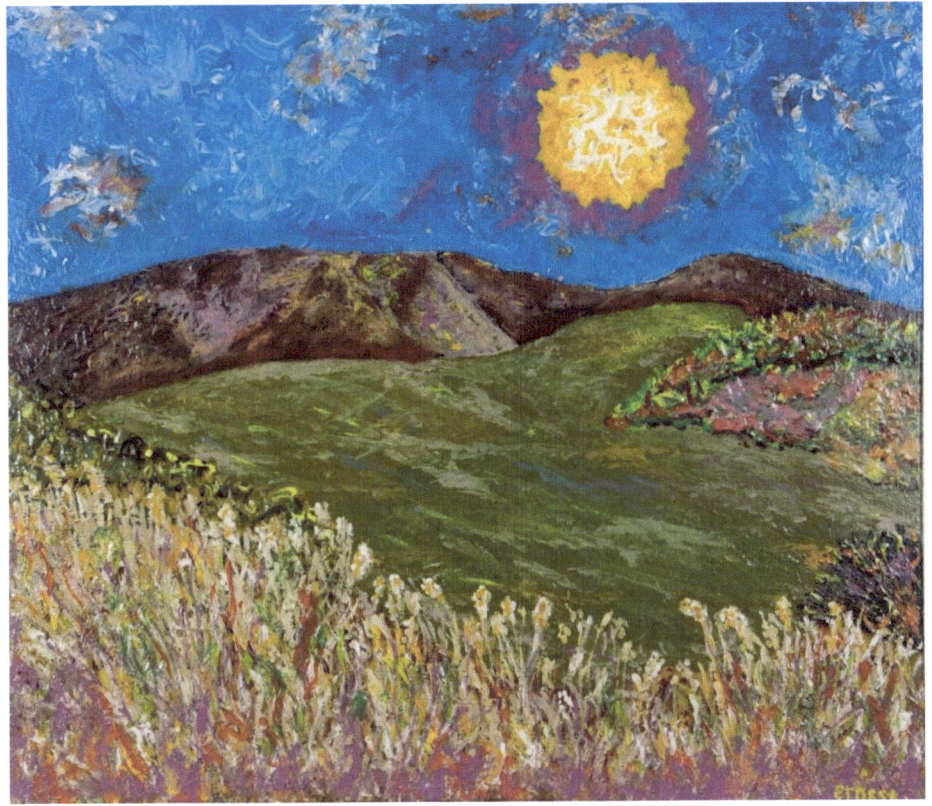

Acrylics on Canvas   30x36

LOST IN ICELAND

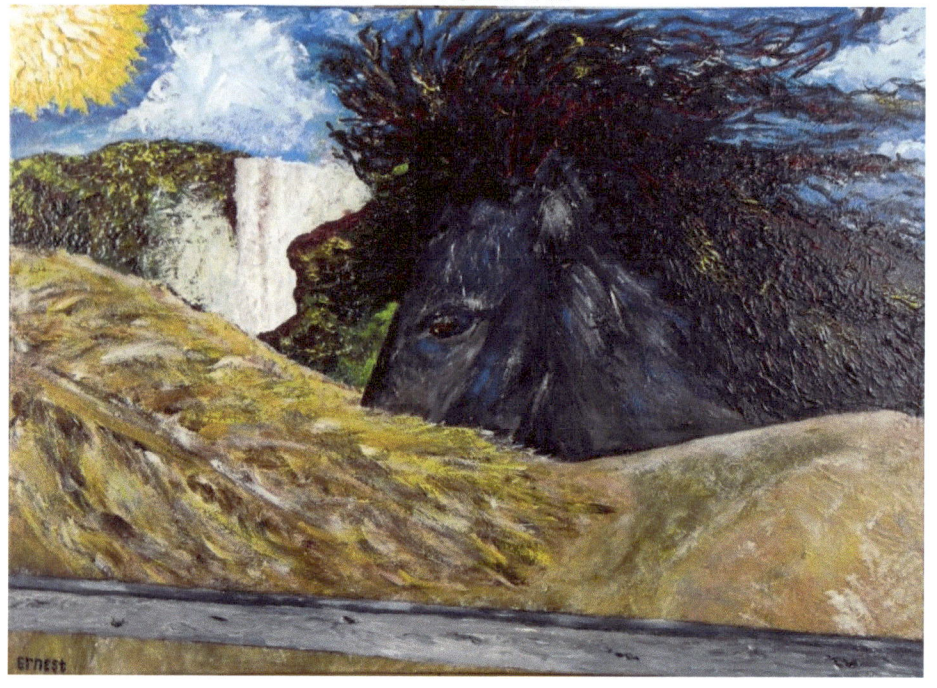

Acrylics on Canvas 24x36

REASON TWO

Ernest paints most every day. Yesterday, he was inspired by one of our photos—a river, a little house, and an Icelandic pony standing up to the fierce wind, his mane in a tailspin. Today he has placed a gessoed 20x30 canvas on the back porch table. He's eyeing a photo of me wearing a dark sweatshirt and shorts standing in the double doorway of the tropically painted condo we rented in Bermuda. I am looking at the lush plantings, a brightly painted little fish house and the jolly bay. My back is to the camera.

"I am going to paint your picture today," he tells me as I leave for my Memoir Group. "My first human being."

"Please don't make me look like the picture of Dorian Gray," I quip.

"Not to worry. I like *pretty* paintings."

I don't say that I don't think the picture he's chosen is especially pretty.

Three hours later when I return the house door is ajar, which surprises me, and Ernest, dressed in a paint-stained old short-sleeve cotton shirt and even more paint-stained shorts, greets me, paintbrush in hand. He has the look of a guy having too good a time.

"Come see your picture, Laurel."

"Uh oh." I'm seeing my picture.

"What's wrong?"

"Well . . . my legs aren't that long. For starters."

"And?"

"You're making me too skinny."

"Overall, you're disproportioned the way Wonder Woman's disproportioned."

"My hair's too dark."

"Hum," he clarifies. "Hair."

"What about my boys? Your girls?"

"So I married a prude."

"You're *disrobing* me!" I wail. "In *public*!"

He shrugs.

"But I do look like that?"

"Yes," he says. "Beautiful."

WINDOW ON THE WORLD

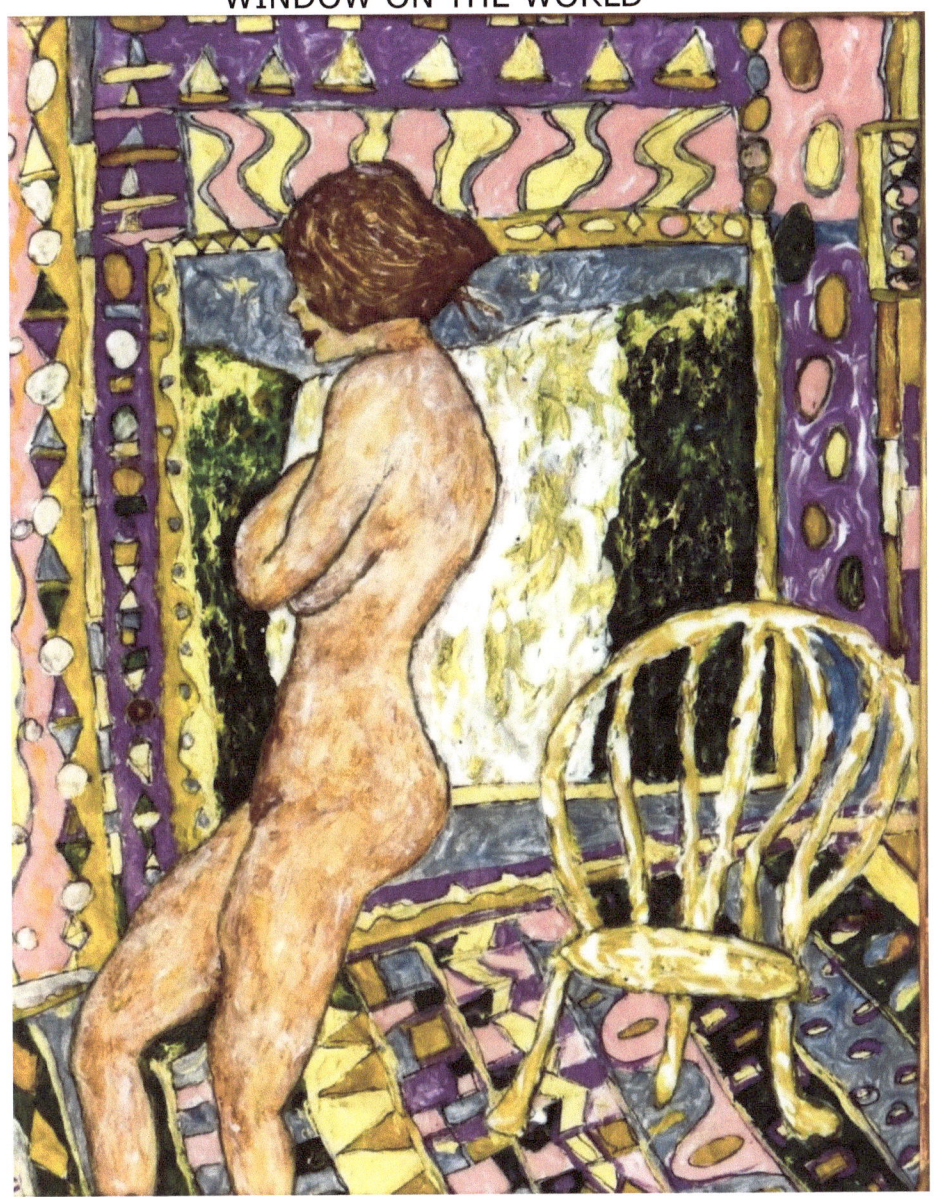

Acrylics on Paper on Canvas 11x17

JEW LANE, TASMANIA

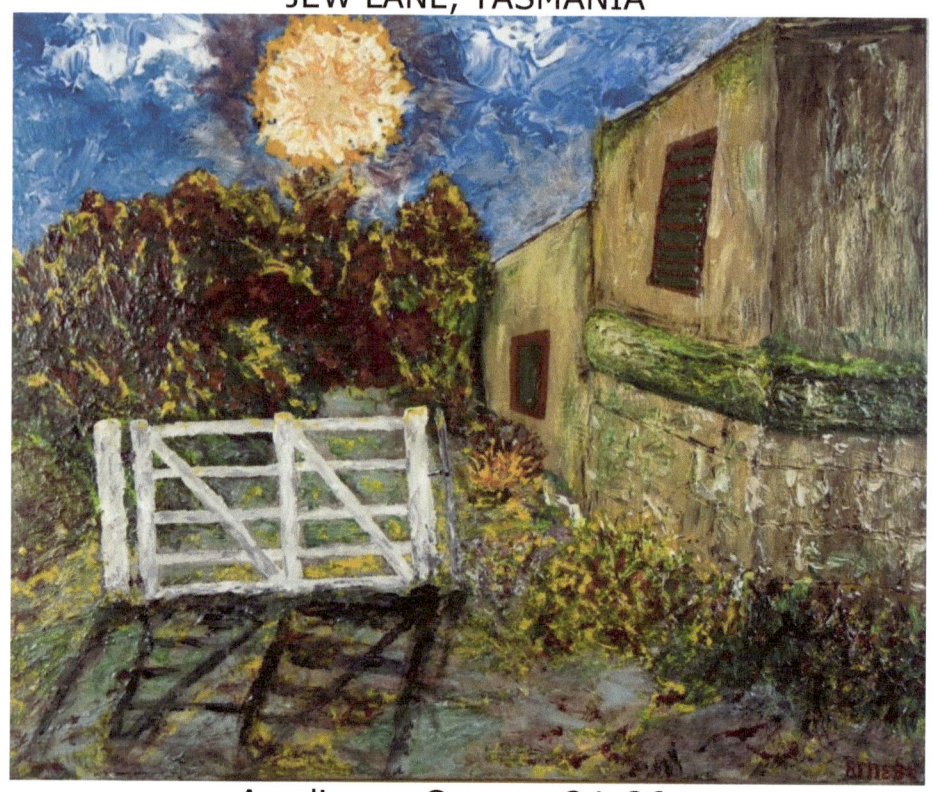

Acrylics on Canvas, 24x36

REASON THREE

Ernest is on the back porch revising "me." I can see "myself" through my study's picture window. Ernest is making my legs even longer and thinner, my skin tone peachier. He is totally absorbed, leaning over the painting, stroking "me" with his favorite brush "I've got it now," I hear him saying to himself. "This looks like her."

And it does.

APHRODITE

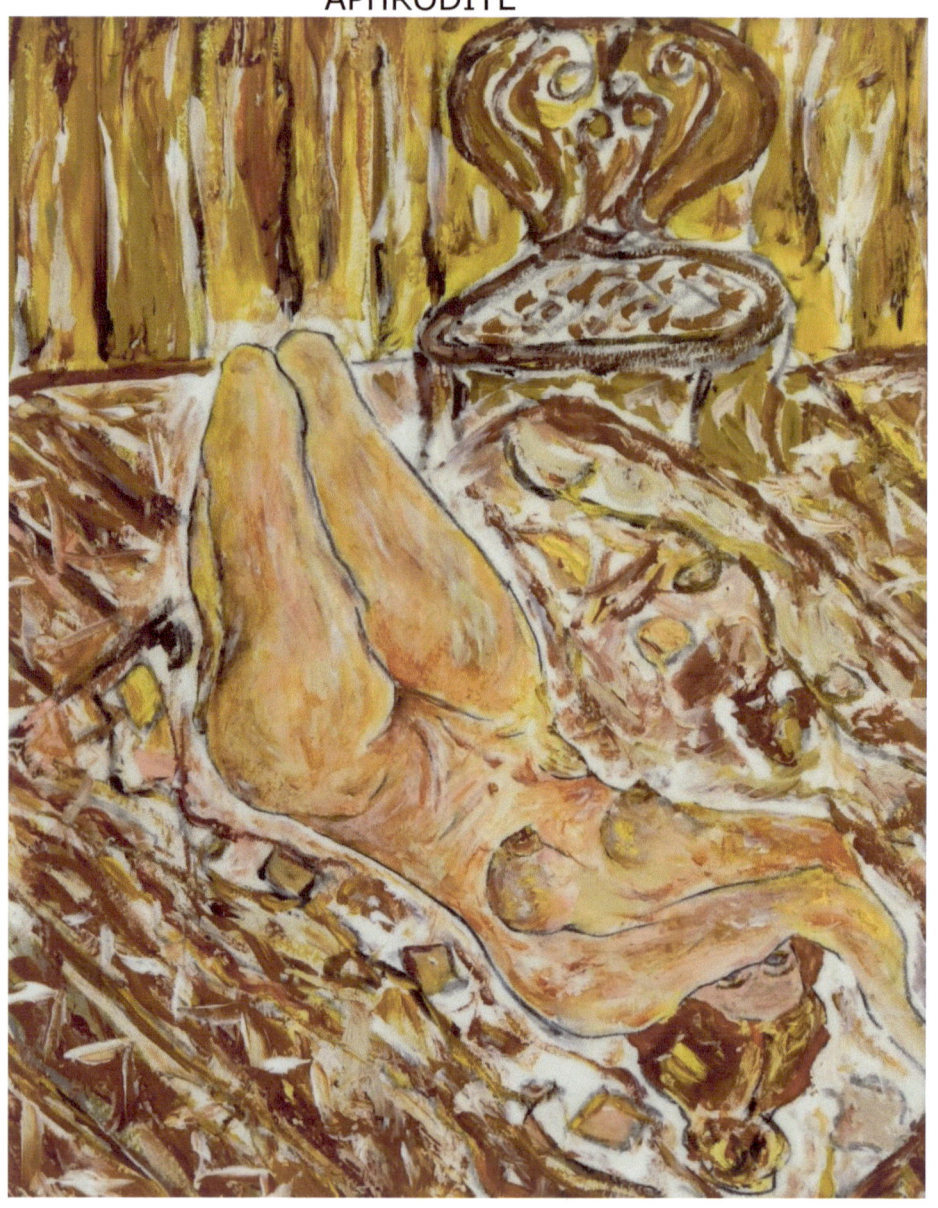

Acrylics on Paper on Canvas 11x17

REASON FOUR

"There's an article in today's *Dispatch*," I say to Ernest as he comes out of his study. "It tells a guy seven ways to be a great husband."

"I saw it," he says.

"And?"

"Real men don't read articles like that."

"Oh?"

"Did it say anything you want to say now?"

"What about that husband's should think of their marriage as one of their jobs?"

"I've been retired for fifteen years," says Ernest.

"That husbands should be at home more."

"I'm at home all the time," he says, which is true. Since taking up up painting he *is* at home all the time—on the back porch, back yard, garage, down in the basement.

"You should pay attention to your wife."

"And here I am!"

"Aim to please her," I persist.

"Yes, dear. I say, 'Yes dear' all the time."

"To your *wife*!"

"And just now I set up your punch line, what more could any wife want?" says Ernest, edging toward the stairs.

We're both doing something that is not on the list: Laughing.

"The problem," he says, "is, wives read too much."

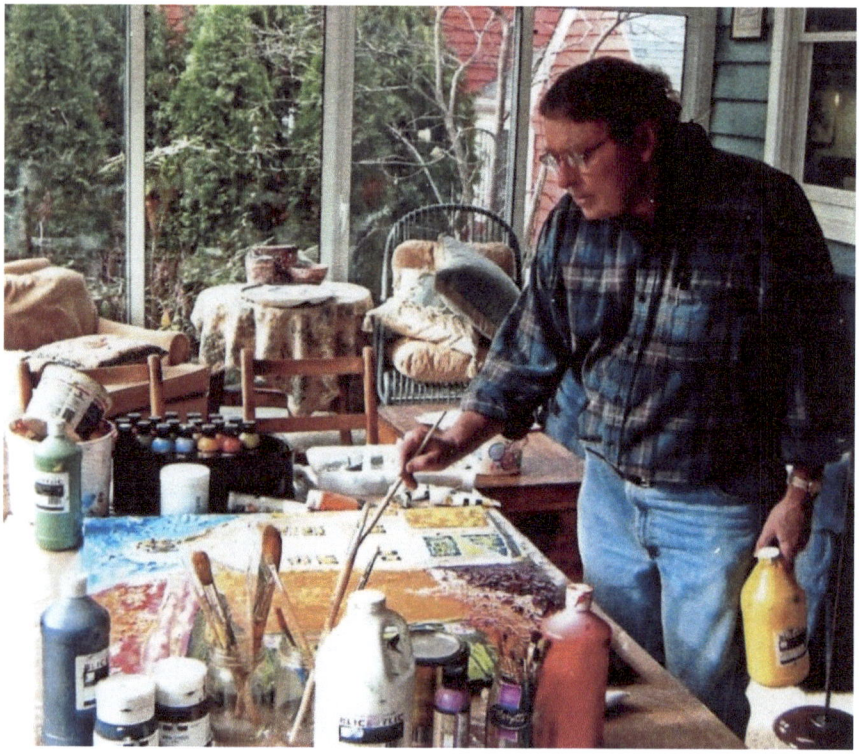

OAK CREEK VILLAGE, SEDONA

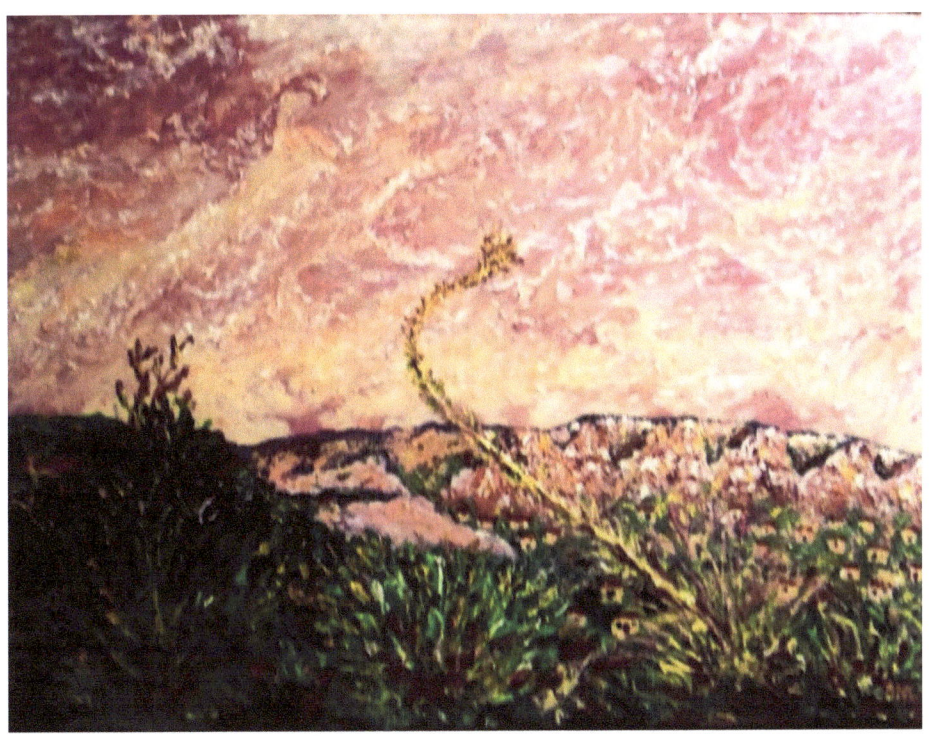

Acrylics on Canvas 16x20

BIG ISLAND, HAWAII

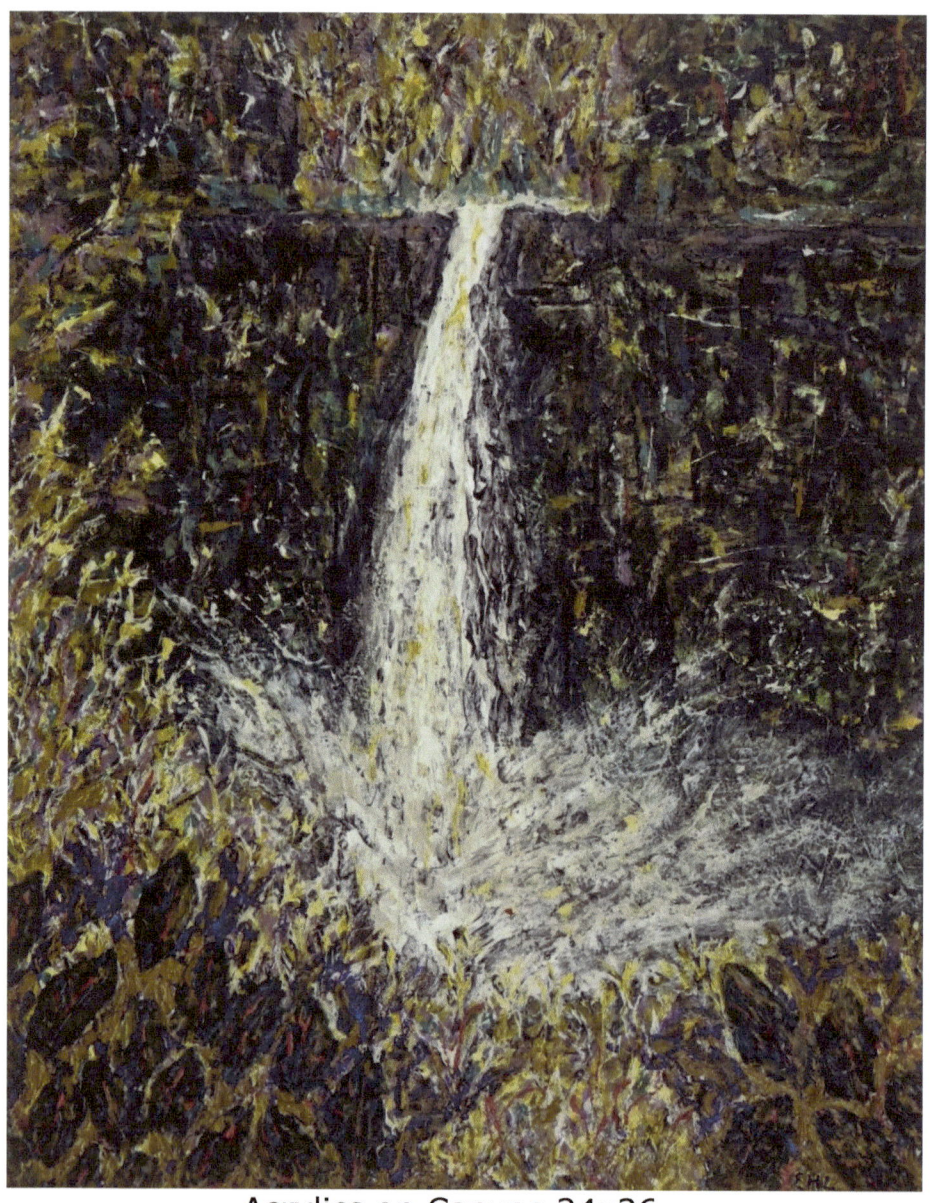

Acrylics on Canvas 24x36

REASON FIVE

On Friday mornings, Ernest paints with the Painters Six-Plus, a group of retired professional men. Their "leader" Bill is an award-winning watercolorist and pastel-artist. He's committed to teaching these men he's chosen to join his group how to paint. When the weather is good, they paint outdoors;when it's lousy they set up their easels and tables in his basement studio.

For this Friday, Bill has told the men to bring a photo of a flower to paint on a small canvas. It's a cold day and they'll be painting inside in the small space. Ernest has chosen two photos—a scraggly little bloom aside a rock in Sedona and a bright red waxy Hawaiian flower with a gigantic stamen, dangling.

"Are those what you want to paint?" I ask.

"Well, I'm trying to follow directions," Ernest says. Following directions is not one of Ernest's strong points. "Bill probably won't think the Sedona scrub plant is a flower. So, I'll paint the red one."

I go about my morning. And Ernest goes about his. When I get home, I see an eight by ten painting of a seductive looking red flower. Its stamen is erect. Ernest is on the back porch beside himself with anticipation for my coming home. He's holding a yellow index card.

"Listen to what they had to say about my painting," he says.

"Did you have a critique group?"

"Not about *the* painting . . . , about *my* painting."

I'm confused but act as if I understand what he's talking about.

"I've written what the guys said," he says. "As I was painting."

I'm thinking he's becoming an ethnographer, now, too, but I don't say that either. Instead, I turn an upturned nose and cocked head towards him, the astute-listener posture.

"Listen," he says, reading his "field notes":

1) "Boy I wonder what a psychiatrist would make of that!"
2) "How long does it take all that paint to dry?"
3) "No wonder he uses big paint tubes!"
4) "You're using more paint on that picture that I've used in my life!"
5) "Boy that's a BUSY painting!"
6) "Ernest's one of those guys who never knows when to stop painting."
7) "Stop painting already!"
8) "Why don't you start painting on the back of it?"
9) "Now he's starting another one!"

Ernest is laughing. He had taken it all in and found it amusing.

If they'd been talking about me I'd have been crying. Or throwing all that paint on them! "What do they know," I say, defending my husband against the infidels. "I *like* that flower!"

"Of course you would. You're long-legged."

"What does that have to do with anything?"

"Well, the veterinarian in our group said that long-legged women were the horniest."

"What? He said *that*?"

"He says that's what the research says. The pharmacist agreed with him. The physician did, too."

"Why were they talking about that?"

"When they weren't talking about my picture they were doing guy talk."

"And did you join them?"

"Nah. I wouldn't stop painting."

MOON LANDING

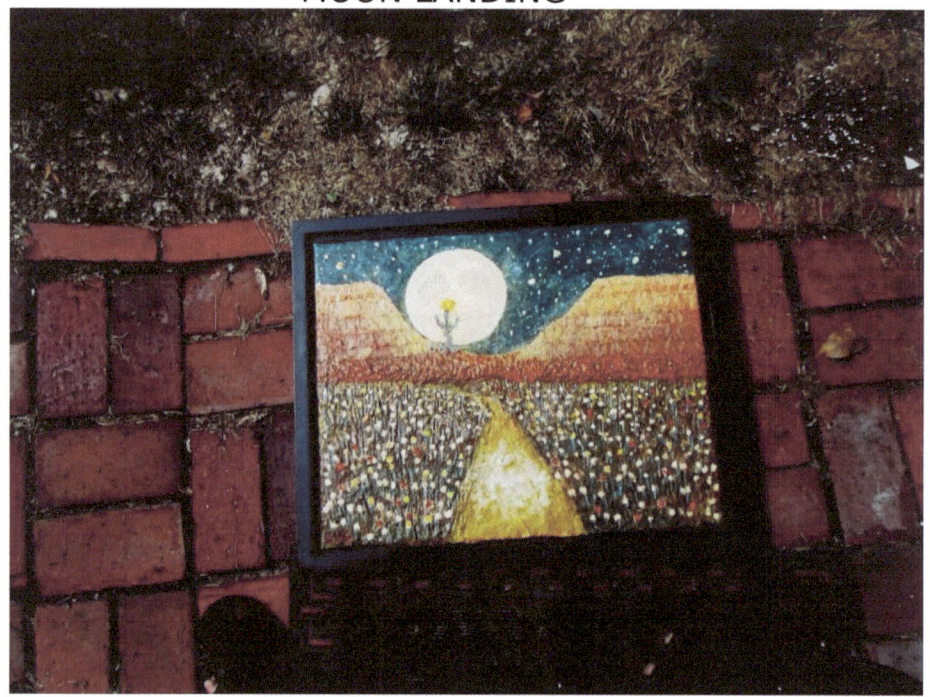

Photograph (16x20) (an *Oil* Painting) by Ernest

REASON SIX

"Oh, Laurel!" Ernest shouts at me. "Oh, no!"

The plastic grocery-store bag I had carried into the kitchen has slipped out of my hands, and its contents splatter the floor.

"I can't help it!" I shout back. Shouting holds back my tears. "You know that!"

The beginnings of arthritis in my hands prevent me from "feeling" whether or not I have a tight grip, especially on plastic and glass. "And it's only going to get worse!"

I leave the kitchen, wiping at my tears of shame, fear, futility.

When I come back, Ernest says, "I'm sorry. You know how sudden noises set me off."

He's put the groceries away and cleaned up the mess.

SEDONA EVENING

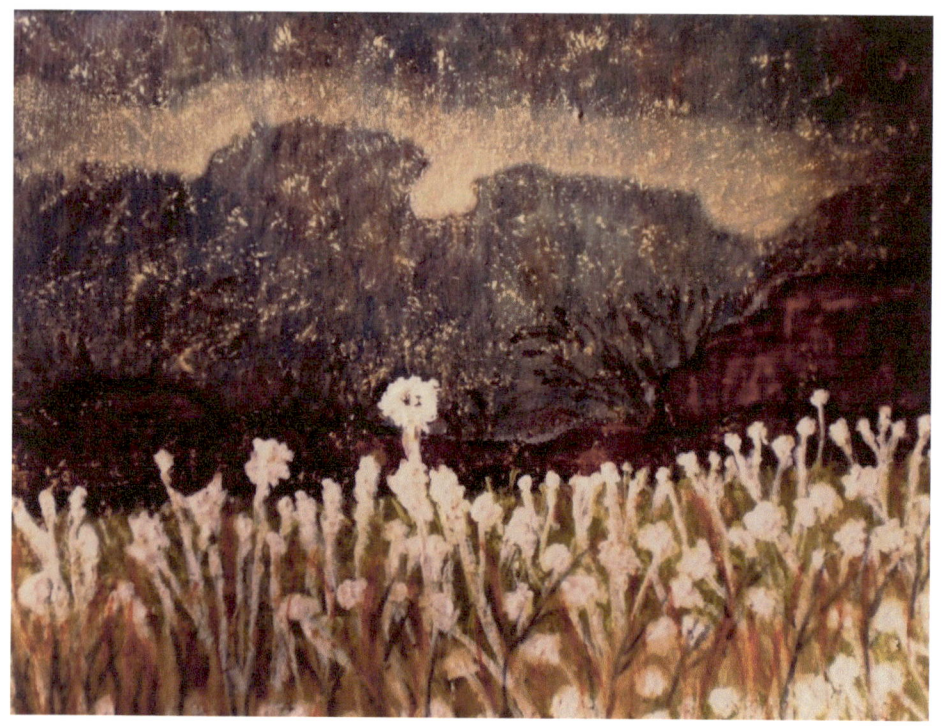

Acrylics on Canvas 16x20

REASON SEVEN

There's paint on my fur-trimmed ice-blue jacket's sleeve. Green paint, black paint, white paint, yellow, red. From the wrist to the elbow. Paint.

"There's paint on my jacket," I say to Ernest matter-of-factly. I'm in a forgiving mood given he has come to the airport in the middle of the night during an ice-storm to pick me up from my vacation in Arizona, and given, too, that he has remembered to bring me my jacket.

"What colors?" he asks, nonchalantly, the soul of innocence.

"Your colors," I say, thinking who else's colors could they be. "Your acrylic paint colors."

"Sorry," he says without a hint of contriteness.

"This is only the ice-blue jacket's second winter and it has only been cleaned once, but it's wearing out already," I say, trying to soften the mini-catastrophe which has less to do with the paint itself but with my plans. I'd been considering returning this unexpectedly poor quality jacket to Nordstrom's, but I can't do that now that it's a coat of many colors.

"I'll do my best to get it off," Ernest says once we're home and he's settled in front of the television set. He catches my questioning look. "It's acrylic. It won't matter if it stays there awhile longer."

Of course it's acrylic, I say to myself. I surely hope he hasn't taken up allergy-inducing oil-paints while I was gone! I tell Mimi about my jacket and she purrs her understanding while I pet her tummy. I do my email and check my snail mail.

"Will you take my suitcases up the stairs?" I call sweetly down to Ernest.

"Be happy to," he says, handing me my jacket all cleaned up.

I follow him up the stairs, turn the corner at the landing and look toward the bedroom. I gasp. Ernest has painted the bedroom while I was gone. The hallway is aglow with color beckoning my spirit. My color. Beach plum. Warm, inviting, luscious, complex latex paint.

DOE MOUNTAIN, SEDONA

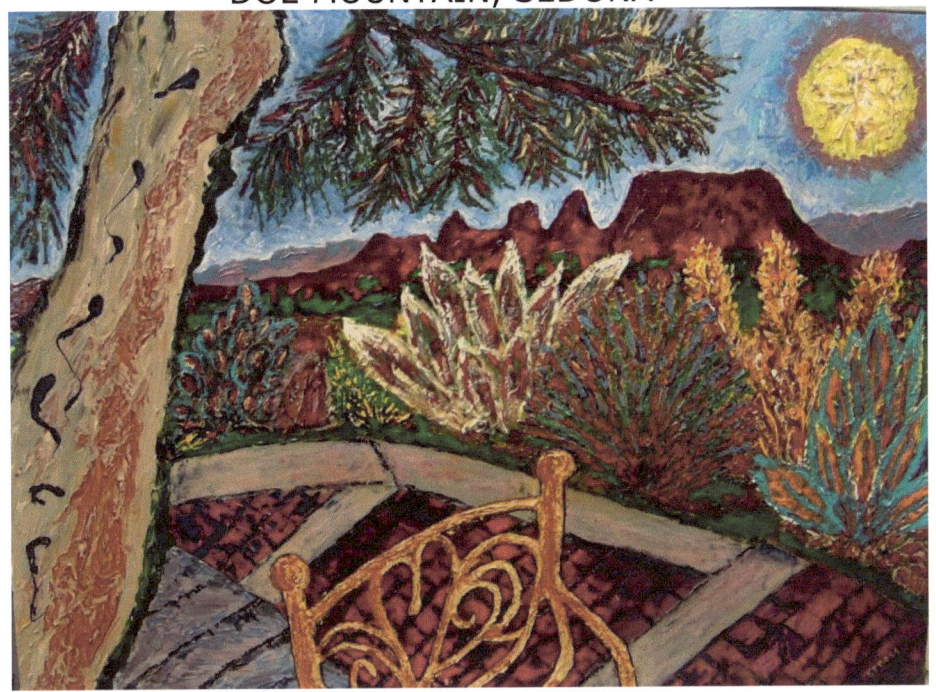

Acrylics on Canvas 36x48

SEDONA SPRING

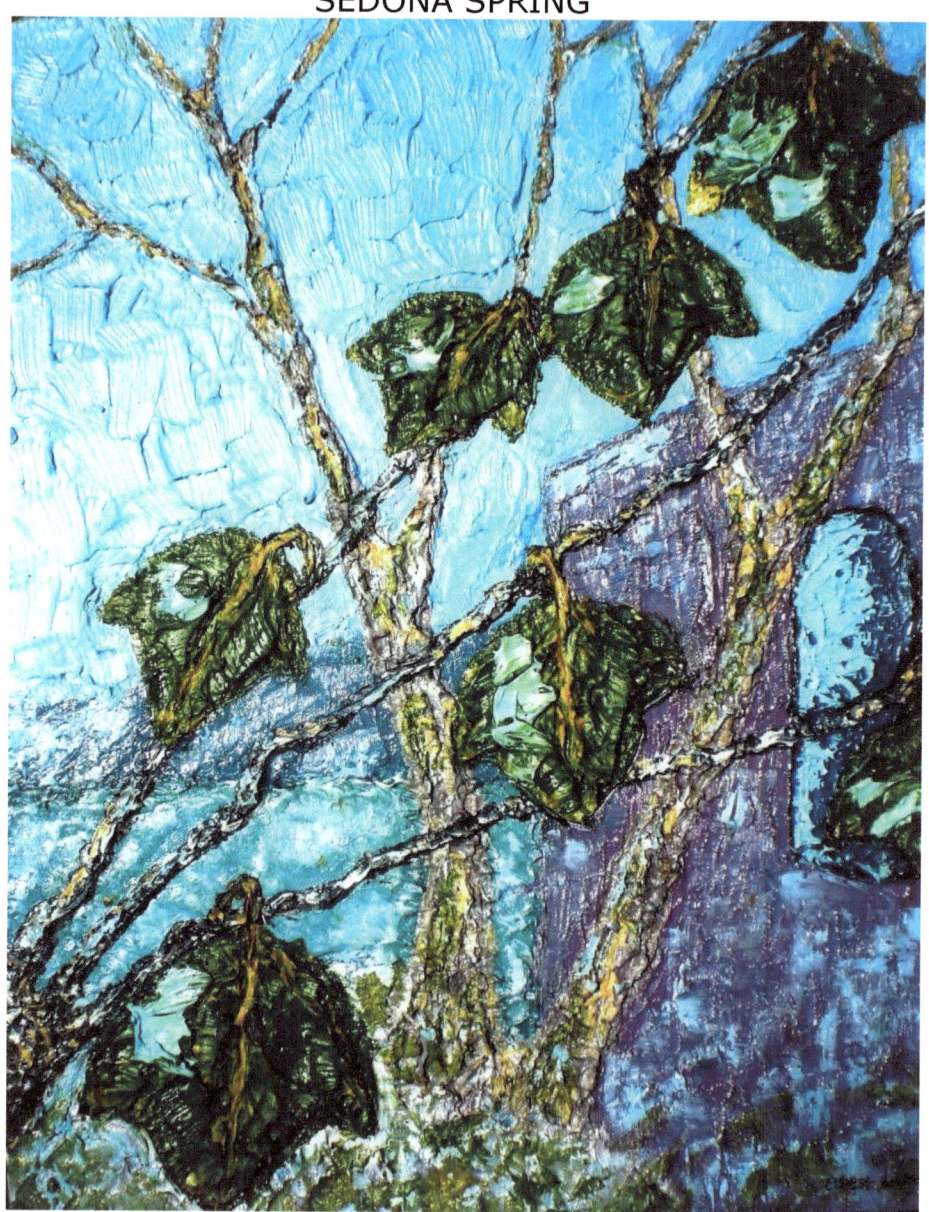

Oil on Canvas 16x20

SEDONA WINTER

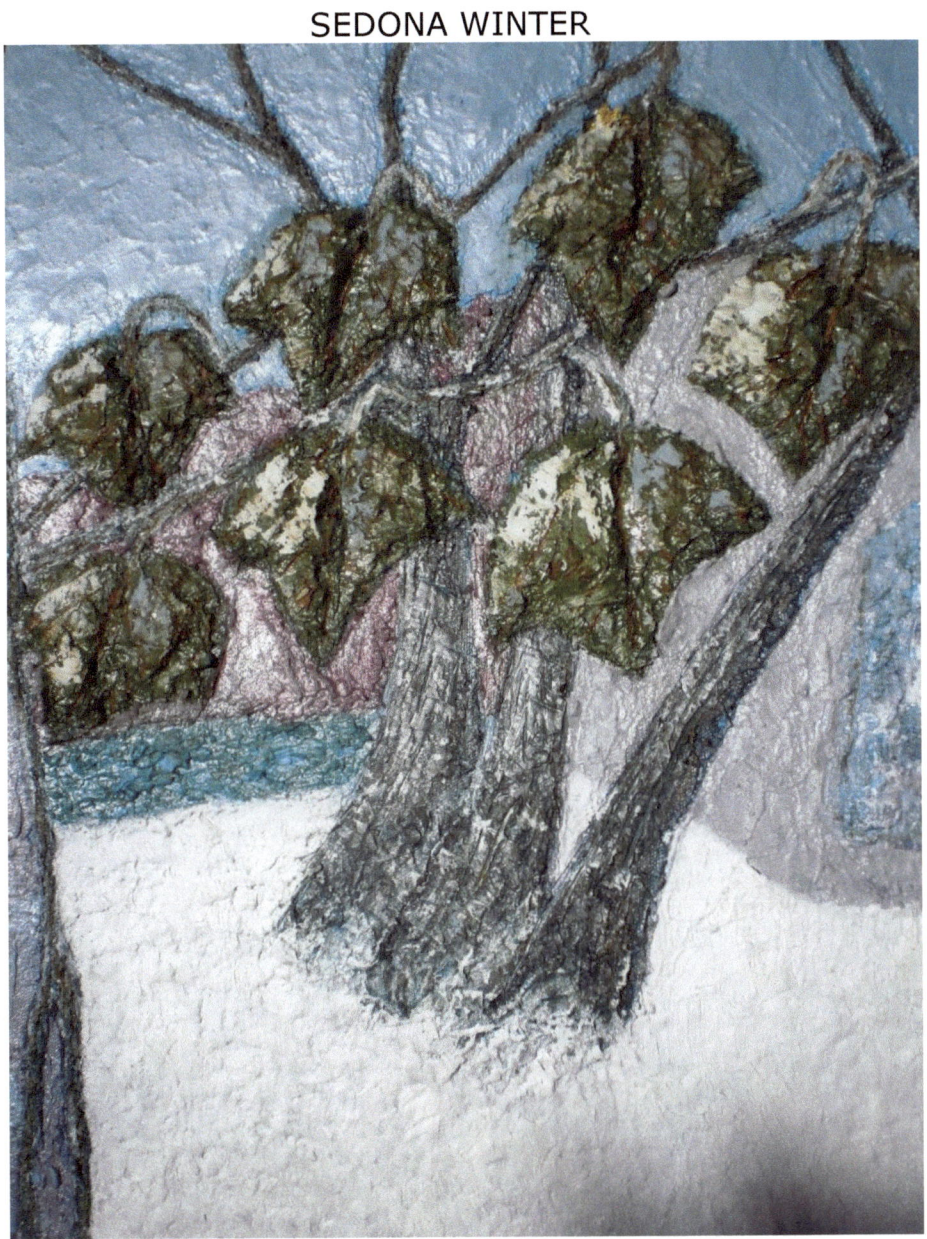

Oil on Canvas 16x20

BY DESIGN

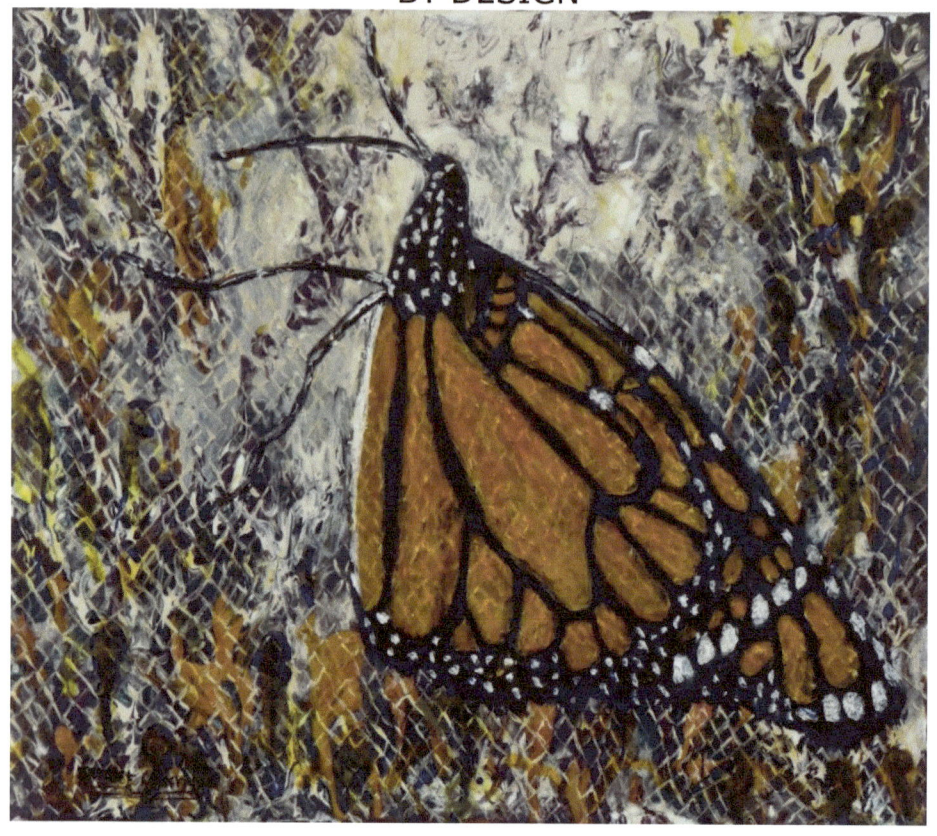

Acrylics on Canvas 24x24

REASON EIGHT

"Not enough room for me to bring wet canvasses up from the workroom," Ernest says, carrying one of his 20x30 acrylics into the kitchen. "The coats get in the way."

I raise my right eyebrow.

"The paint got on the inside of your coat," he says.

I raise my left eyebrow.

"Well, at least it didn't get on *my* coat."

I lower my eyebrows.

"It's an old man's joke," he says.

"If it's an old *man's* joke," I say, "why am I giggling?"

THE FIRE THIS TIME

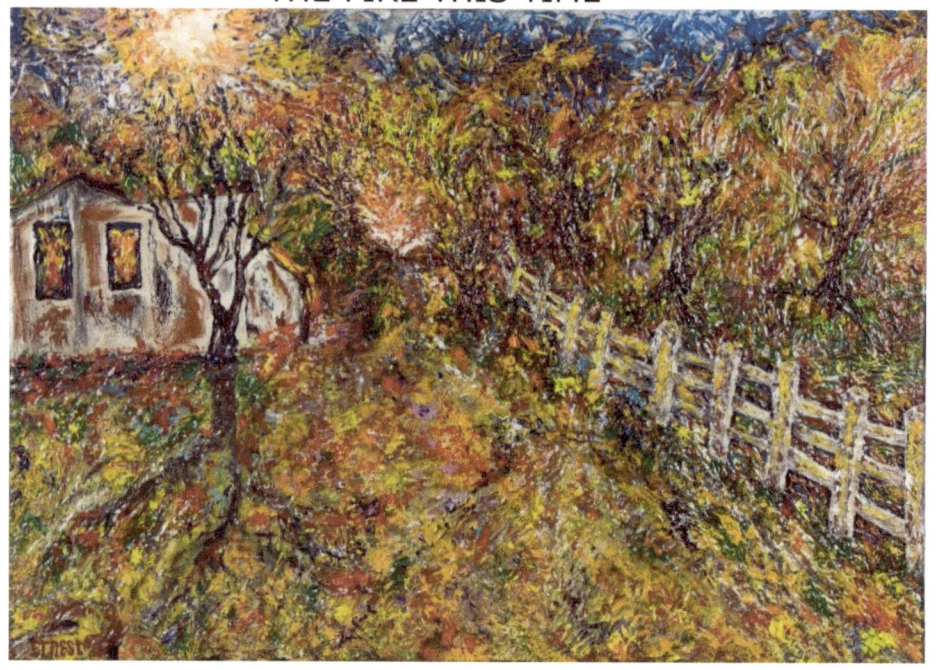

Acrylics on Canvas 24x36

REASON NINE

"It's happened again," Ernest declares at breakfast. He's shaking his head, and maybe his fist behind his back, but about that I'm not sure because he's looking at me straight on. "Some monster comes at night and attacks the hummingbird feeder. Look!" he cries, pointing out of the sun porch window.

I look out and see, yet again, our bright red hummingbird feeder on the ground and the wrought iron rod that holds the feeder above the ground at our eye level, once again, tortured and twisted and leaning against the double-pane glass.

"It's definitely not that black and white cat that stalks our yard," I say.

"Grendel's mother." He rolls back the patio glass door. "Great heroism is called for!" he calls out heading into the yard in his sleeping shirt and his Crocs. He unbends the crooked iron rod and brings the feeder into the house.

"We're just about out of sugar, too," he laments. "We've been feeding some sucrose-addicted beast . . . 'My baby don't need no shuga . . . ,'" he croons a little blues ditty as he prepares the hummingbird homemade nectar, fills the feeder, brings it outside and hooks it back on its holder. We settle into breakfast on the porch watching hummingbirds. Our favorite little green one eyes us, and with a flick or two or five-hundred of its wings thanks Ernest for its repast.

The scene is played over again every morning for nearly a month.

Then, one evening, just at dusk, Ernest is looking at the back yard and calls to me, "Come look!" He has spotted the monster that attacks the birdfeeder—the most obese raccoon we have ever seen, bigger than we could ever have imagined.

"It's an Ohio raccoon, all right," I say, referring to our state's being number one in the fat department.

"I'll have to take in the feeder at night from now on," Ernest says, which he does.

Minutes later he has filled a pie pan with our dinner leftovers. I watch him as he puts the goodies under the iron rod.

"It's good to recycle," Ernest says, coming in, looking pleased. "What shall we name him, ah . . . her?

TASMANIAN DEVIL

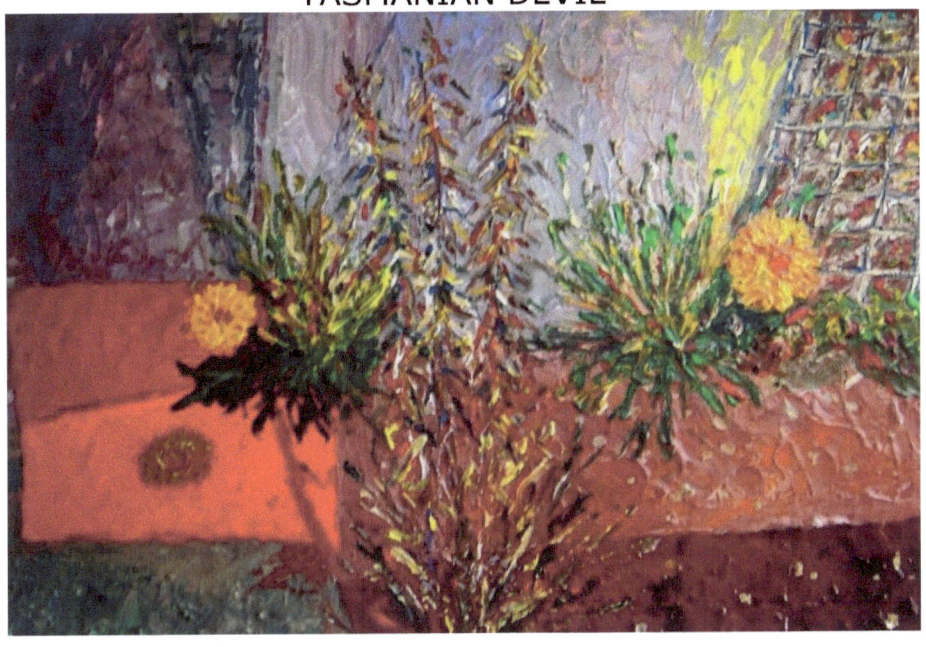

On the Bridge to Port Arthur Prison, Tasmania
Acrylics on Canvas 16x20

BELL ROCK MIRAGE, SEDONA

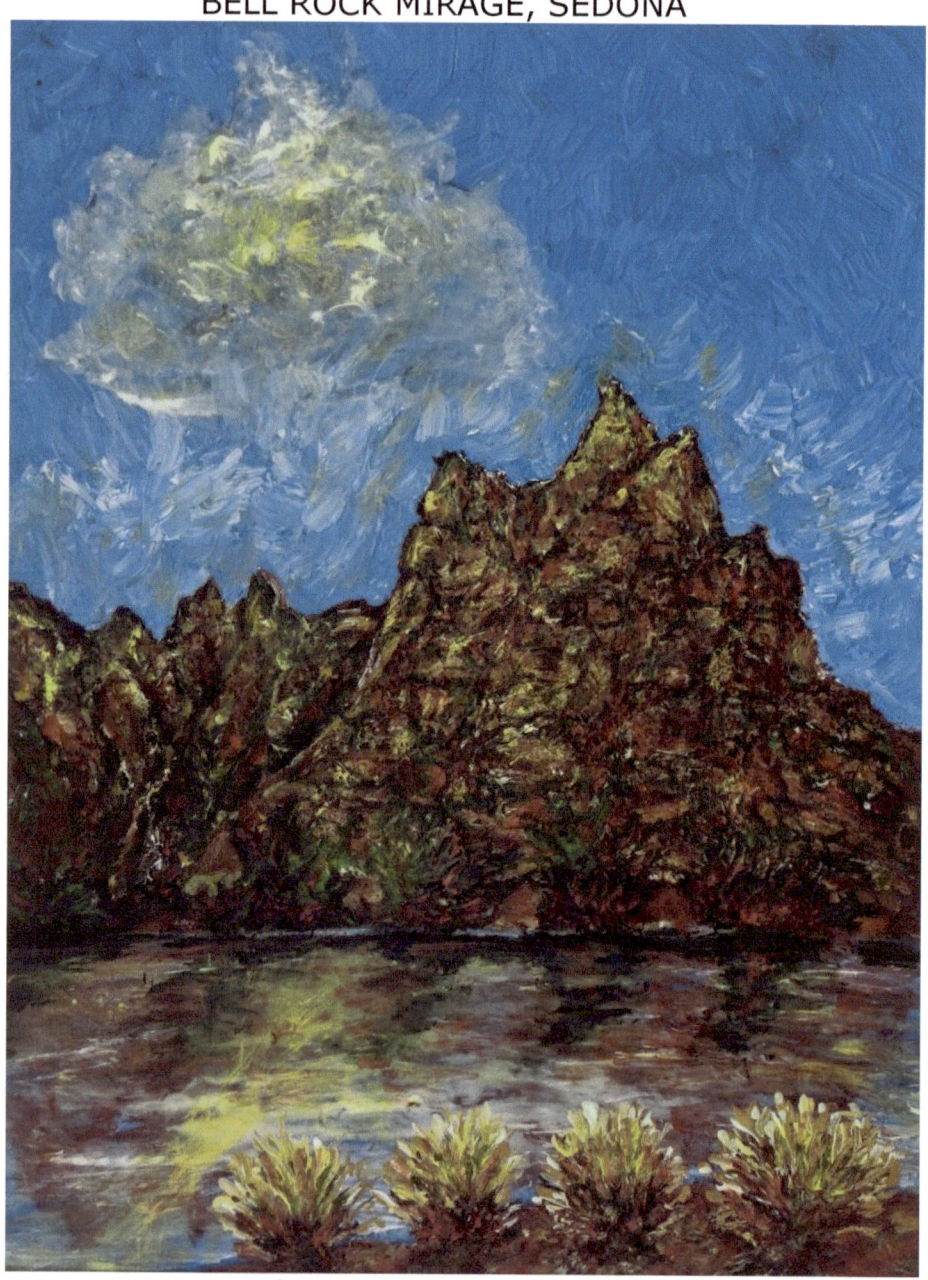

Acrylics on Canvas 24x36

REASON TEN

My plan is to have the high desert vortex energy in Oro Valley, north of Tucson seduce Ernest and lift him up, as it has me in the past, so that he'll want, as I do, a winter home here. We spend a week in August, there, hiking in the Coronado National Forest, driving from cacti to pine forest up Mount Lemmon, descending into the Titan Missile site, now a privately run museum, escaping the monsoons that have flooded Saguaro Canyon, eating cherries and juicy steaks on our pretty little patio watching the sun set over the Catalina mountains.

We are at perfect ease with each other and the world.

With sadness, I drive him to the airplane at the end of "his" week. I'll be staying another week--to see how I "do" alone.

I am lonely. Immediately. I wait for Ernest's phone call.

"Hi," he finally calls. "I'm home. I love you."

"I love you, too," I say. "I miss you. How was your flight?"

"Great. There was almost no one on it, so I sat by the window." Usually, he sits on the aisle.

"I was looking out," he continues,"and everything in nature looked beautiful . . . And then, I had this 'Ah ha!'"

"Yes?"

"--Everything is beautiful. Everything in nature . . . "

"Hmm . . . "

"—and everything humans have made, too."

I am smiling.

"'Beauty is truth, truth beauty.'" He is quoting Keats. "'That is all ye know on earth, and all ye need to know.'"

I catch my breath.

"I didn't understand those words before," he continues. "But now I do."

"Nice."

"Yep. Pretty darn uplifting."

TEETH OF THE LION

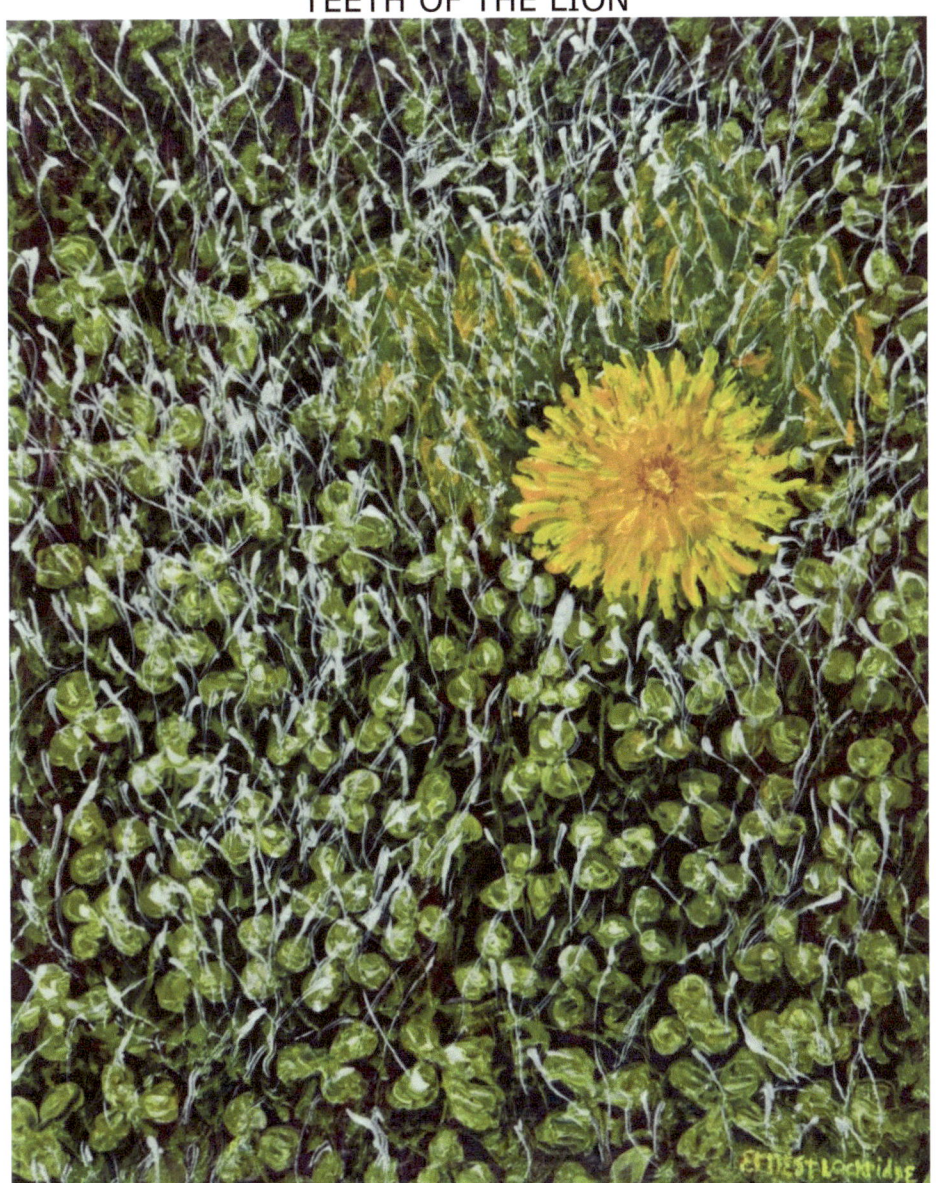

Acrylics on Canvas 16x20

"ARE WE THERE YET?"

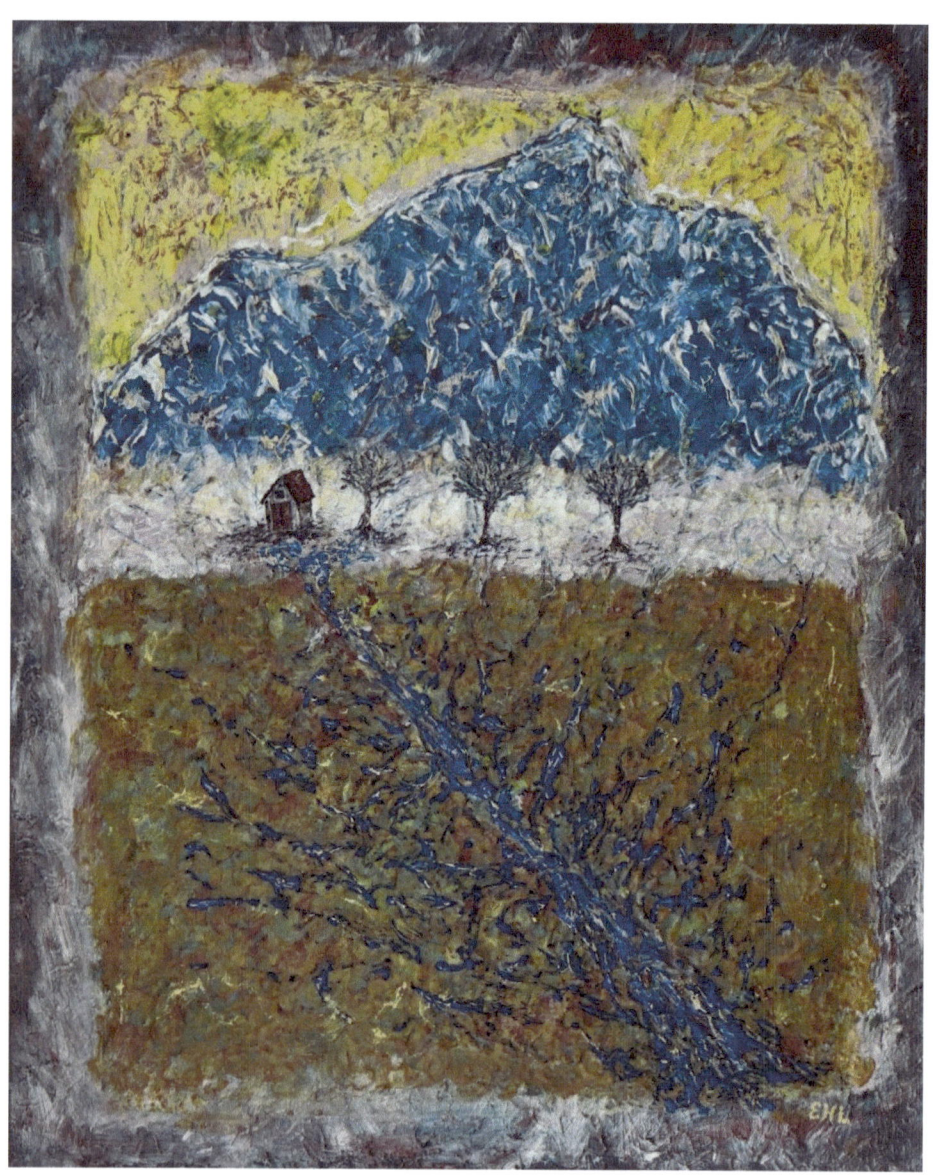

Acrylics on Canvas 24x36

CONVERGENCE

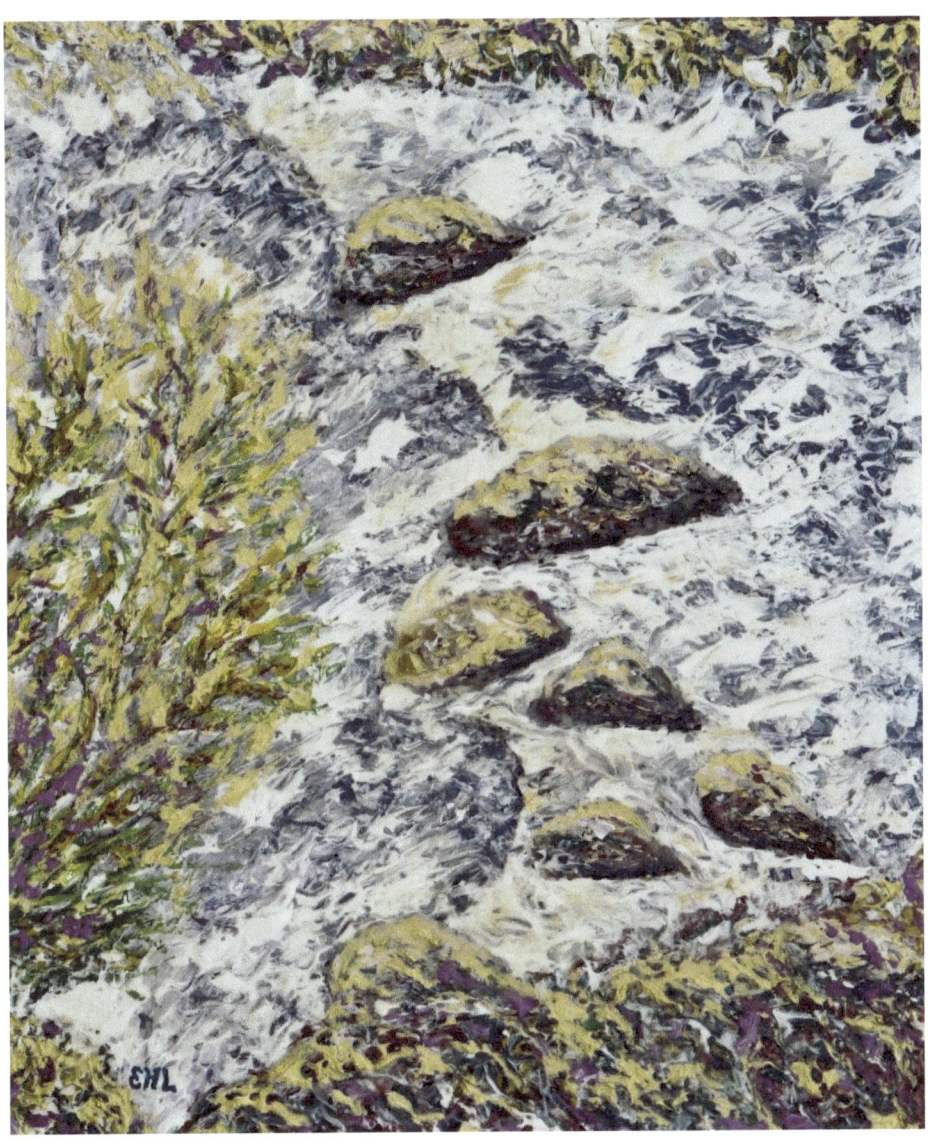

Acrylics on Canvas 24x36

EN CARMARGUE

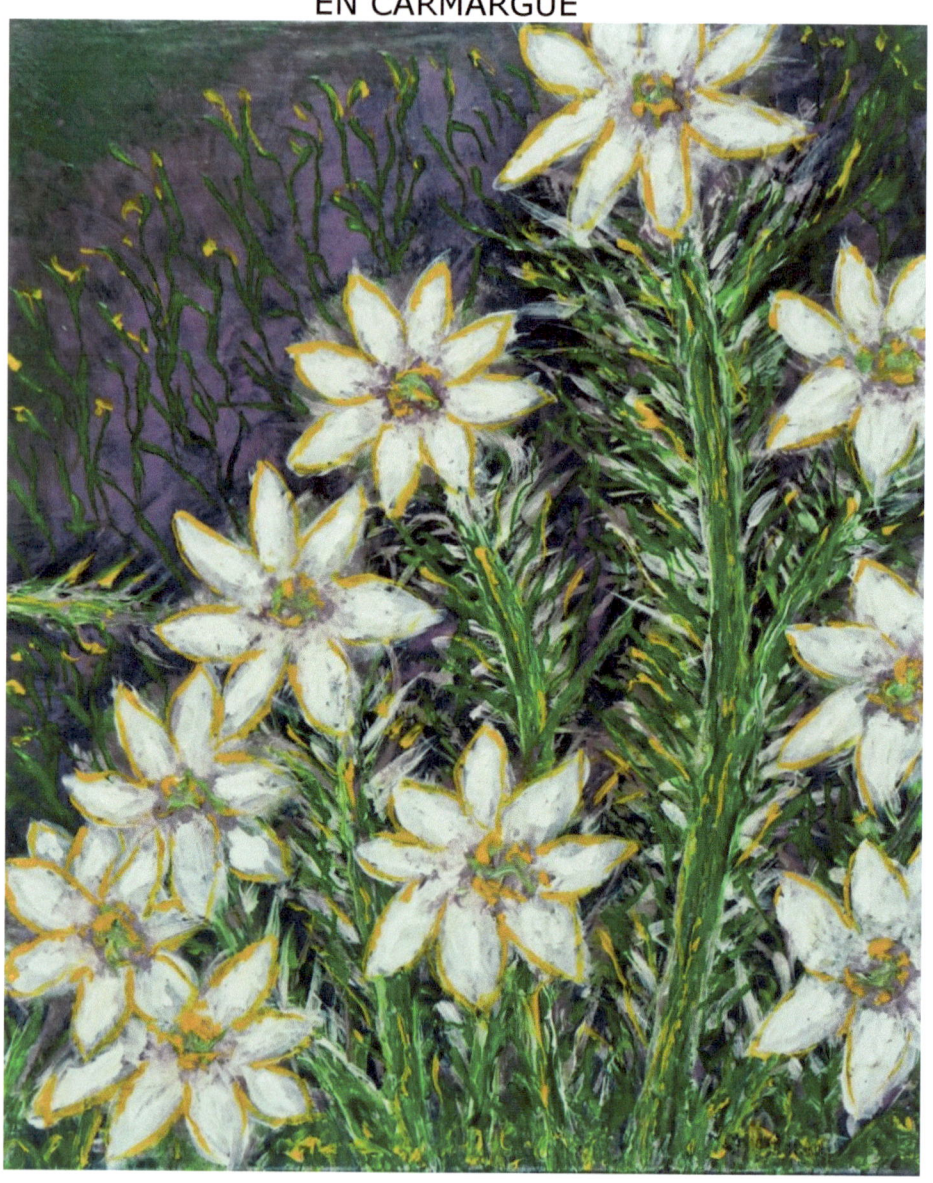

Acrylics on Canvas 16x20

REASON ELEVEN

I am in Chicago at the National Communication Association's convention, where my recent book is being honored. I am not a member of the organization or a "communicationist"—I think that's what they must be called, or should be, anyway. On the last afternoon of the conference my feelings of loneliness and disconnection get the best of me and I decide to attend a session for theater teachers. Why not?

Fourteen of said teachers have volunteered to present five-minute acting exercises. We acting teachers--or those such as me who are acting as acting-teachers—sit in a large circle and the exercises begin: We breathe in energy, breathe out energy; we come forward, touch each other and make "story shapes" with our bodies; we tell a back-story for a favorite character; we bend and twist and shout.

And then, a Square-pants-Bob-looking guy asks us each to stand by our chair. Through body "reshaping" we are to become another person. "Start with your feet first," he says. "Are they pointed in, pointed out, light, grounded?"

I turn my feet out, and settle into that unfamiliar stance.

"What about the hips?" he asks.

I raise my right one, lower my left one, bending my knees slightly. I feel a tug around my ribs as I do so.

"The back? Shoulders?" he asks.

I stretch out my upper back. The shoulders are larger and stronger now.

"Head? Face?"

I cock my head slightly forward, square my jaw, raise my eyebrows, widen my eyes, look intent."

"And your arms and hands?"

I put my left hand in my jeans' pocket, and in my right one I hold a painting brush. I reach out to my canvas, and paint.

"Nice brush strokes," Square Pants says.

"Thanks," I say. And give a hearty laugh. I have "become" Ernest, and no longer feel disconnected and lonely.

"HAVE SIGHT OF PROTEUS RISING FROM THE SEA"

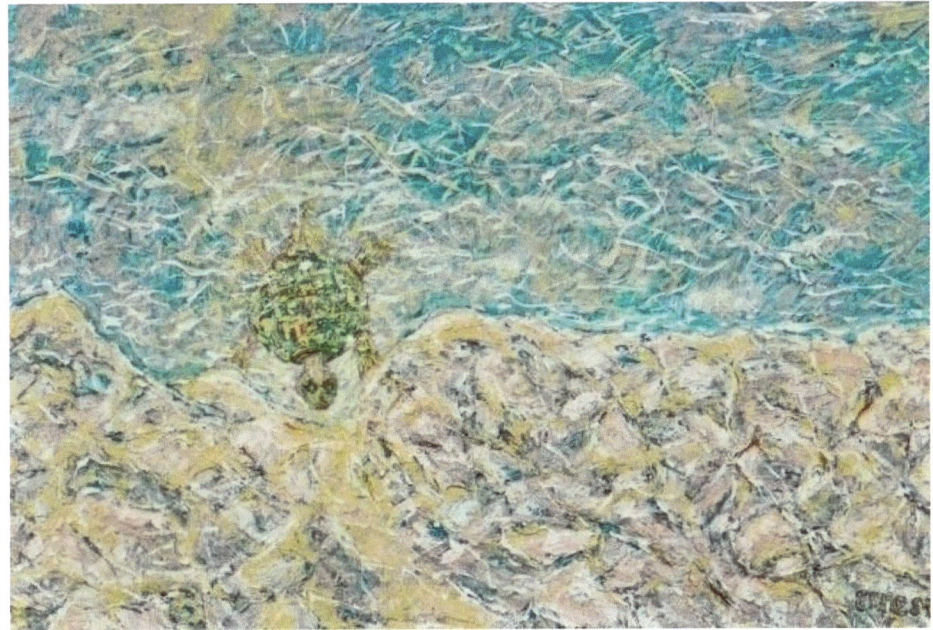

Acrylics on Canvas 24x36

TIDAL POOL, HAWAII

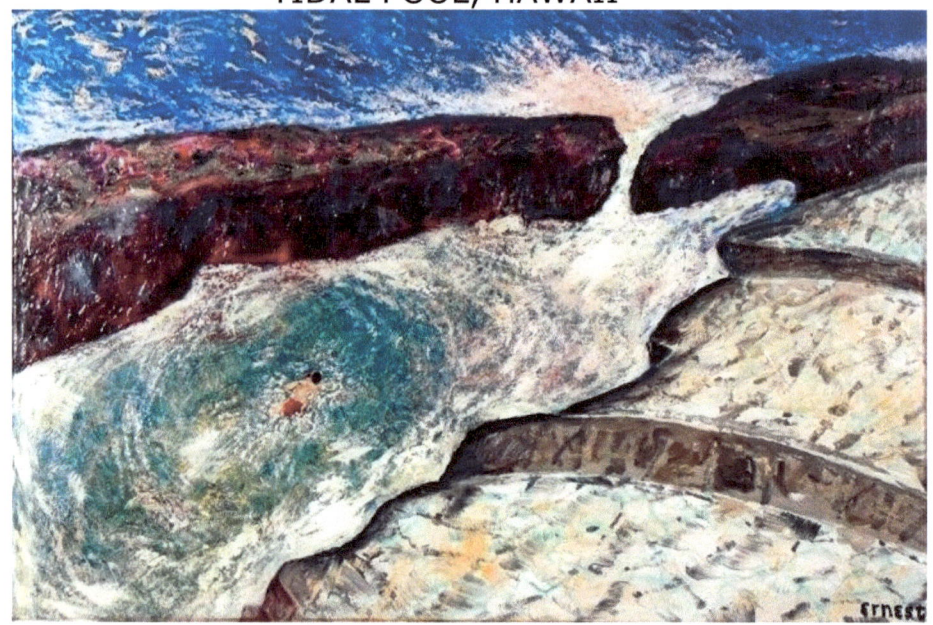

Acrylics on Canvas 24x36

ROMAN THEATER, ARLES

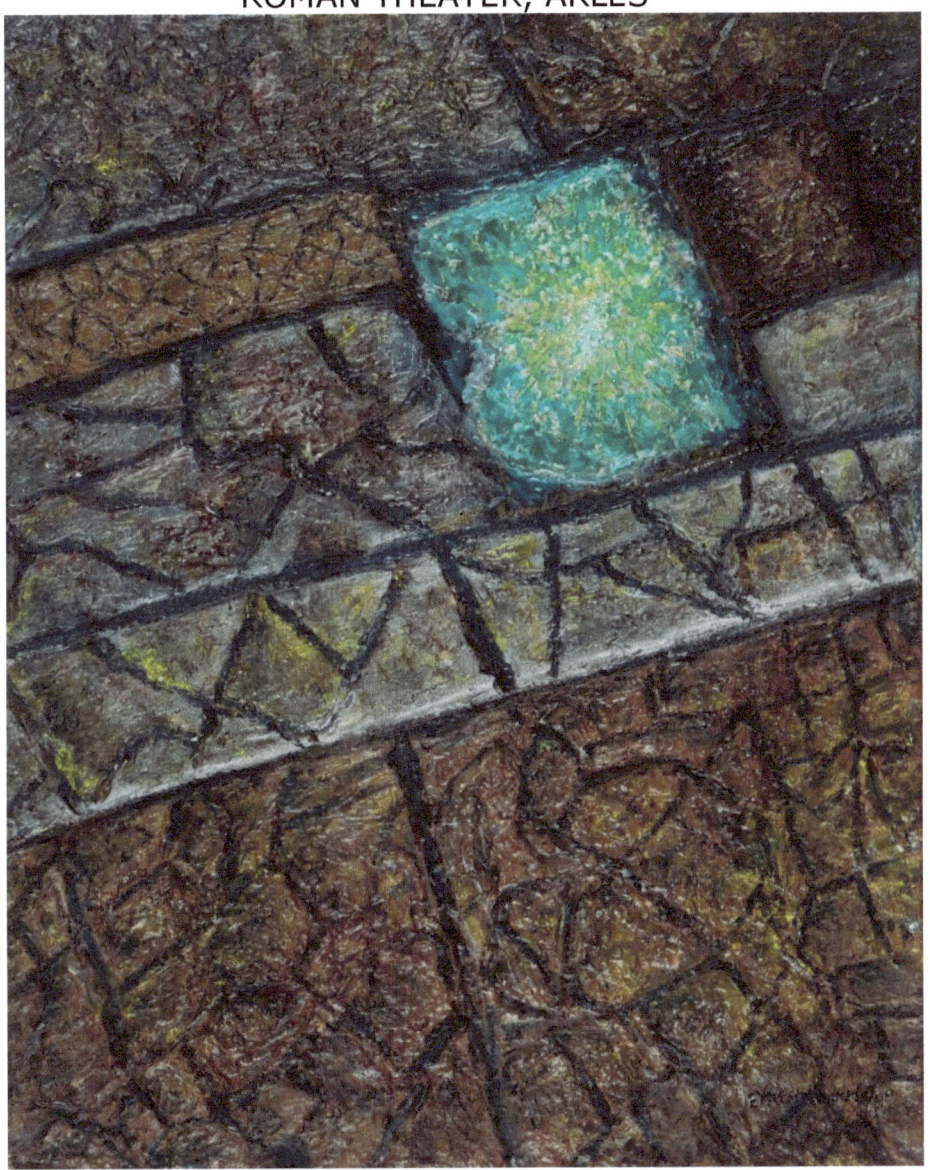

Acrylics on Canvas 16x20

FRONDS

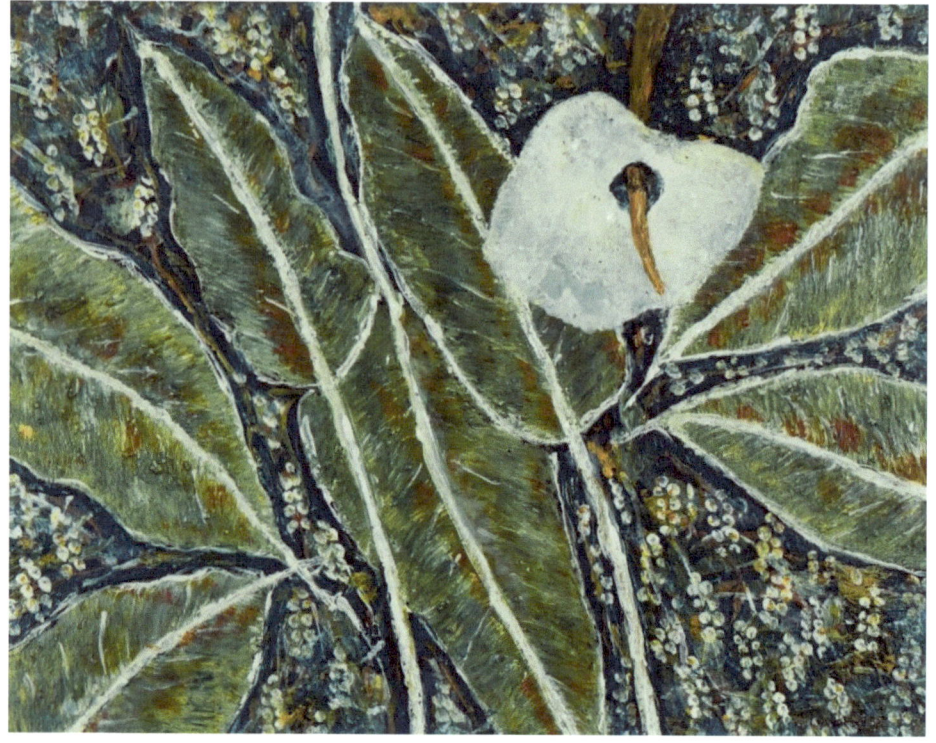

Acrylics on Canvas 26x24

REASON TWELVE

Ernest's solo-show at Northwood ArtSpace opens, and the room fills up with friends and strangers. The walls are alive with Ernest's vivid acrylics, simultaneously comforting and stimulating. People admire them and admire him. It is his night.

My new friend Elaine comes in. Elaine lives on the other side of town.

"Elaine! Hi!" Am I shouting? I know I am being effusive, much more so than my usual calming demeanor. I had no idea she would be here. "Come, meet Ernest," I say, taking Elaine by the hand to where Ernest is holding court.

"I love your wife," Elaine says.

Not a moment passes before Ernest says to Elaine, me, and the court, "I love her, too."

PENELOPE

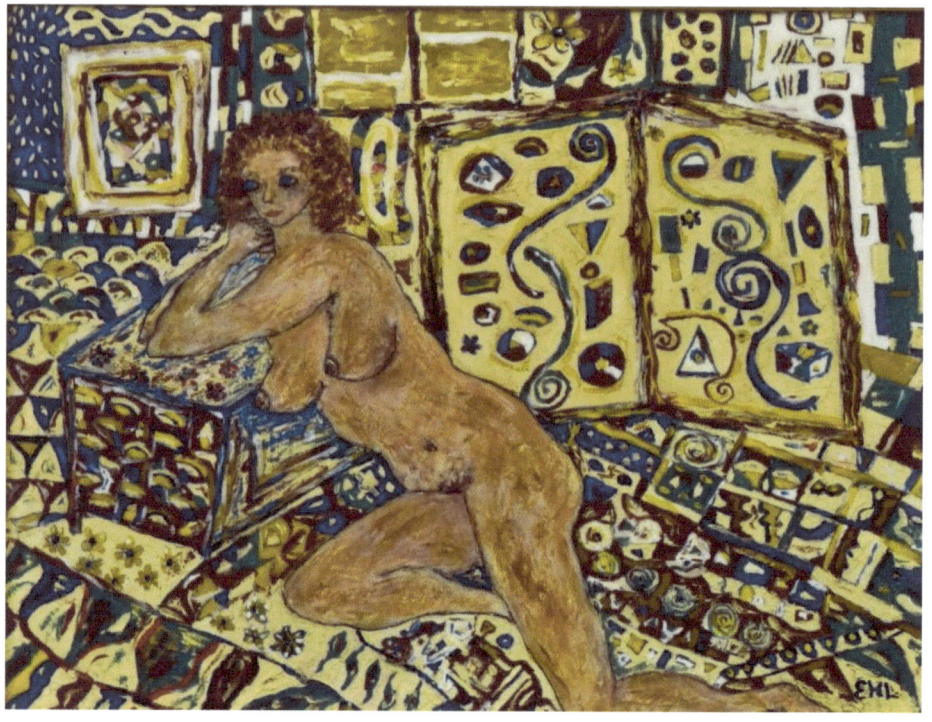

Acrylics on Paper on Canvas 11x17

REASON THIRTEEN

Ernest's *Artist Statement*:

Still Life is a contradiction in terms. Nature is kinetic, overflowing with living design. By mimesis and imagination the artist participates organically in this ongoing Creation.

HONEY PATCH

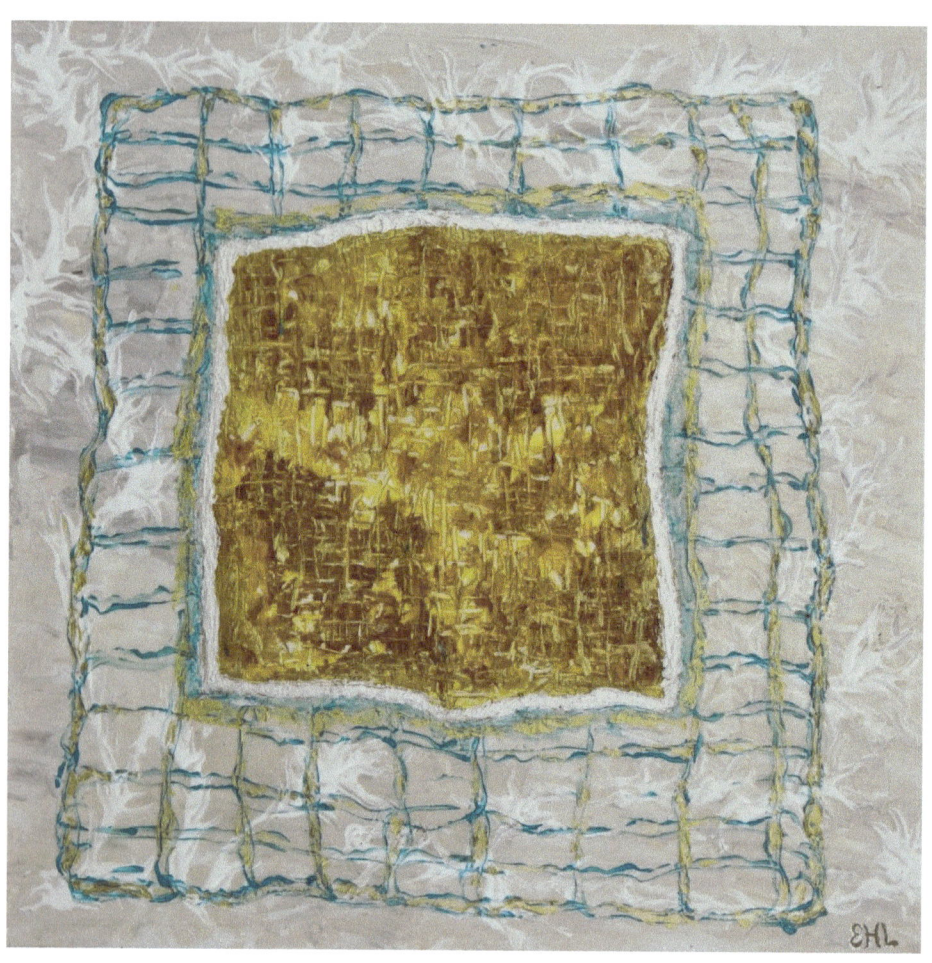

Acrylics on Canvas 24x24

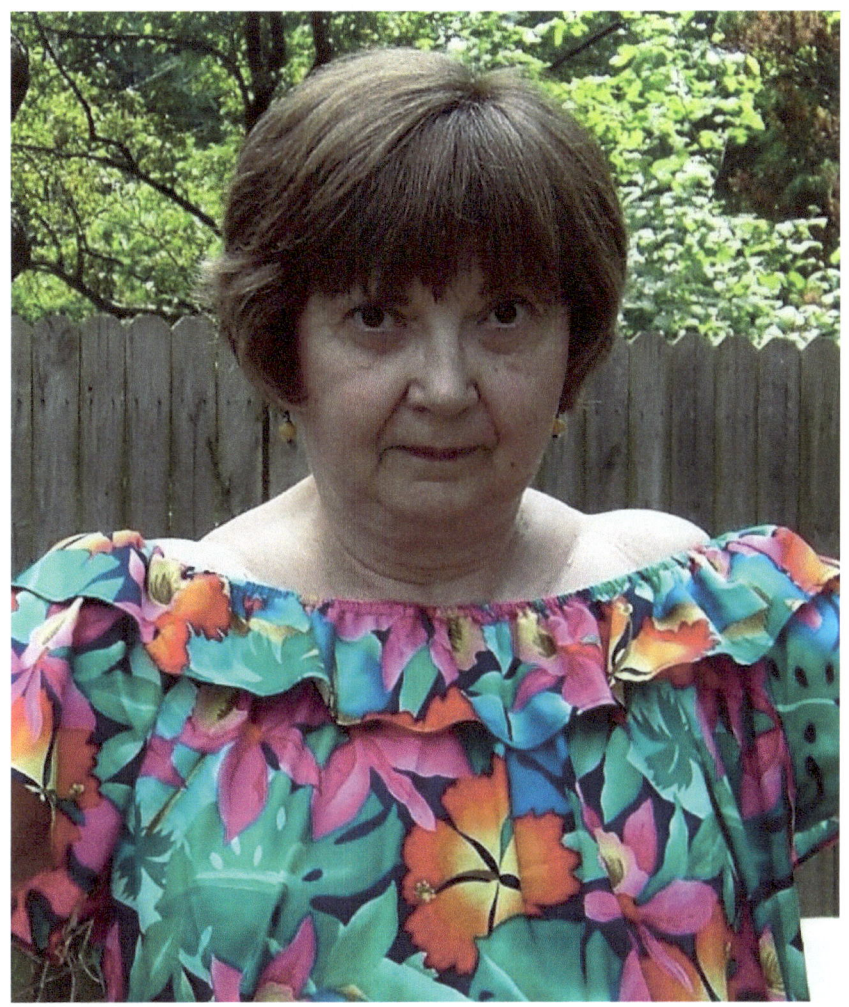
Laurel

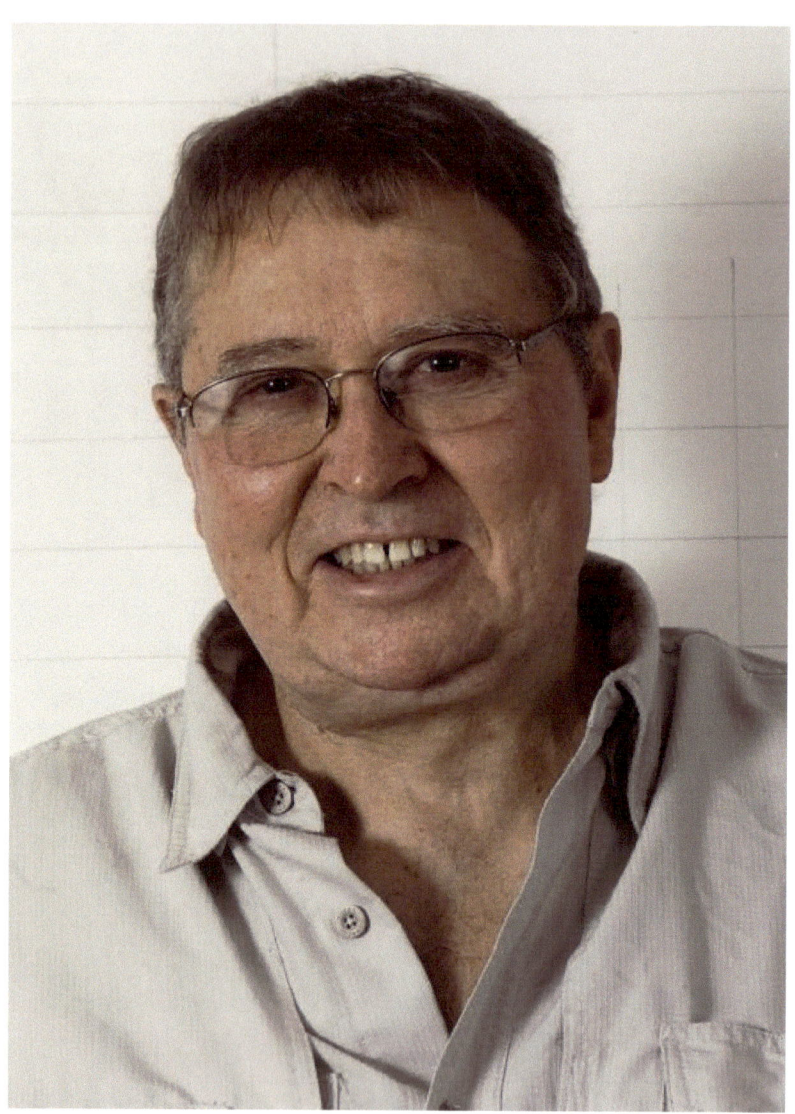

Ernest

VALEDICTORY

Every morning I sit at the same place at our round oak table, a place that gives me a view of the only wall in the kitchen, a wall we once thought we would open-up with a picture window but, thankfully, decided not to.

Every morning I see Ernest's paintings on that wall.

Different paintings.

So, it is as if I wake up each morning to a gallery--perhaps one I have not seen before, or perhaps not seen how the collection works together. Not only do I engage in a visual adventure, I engage in an emotional one, too. Some of the paintings remind me of places we've been, when we were younger; others remind me of places I have been in my heart. Sailboats; Moon-landings; Sedona-scapes . . . And the Sun. Almost always, the Sun.

This is a very good way to start the day.

PORTAL

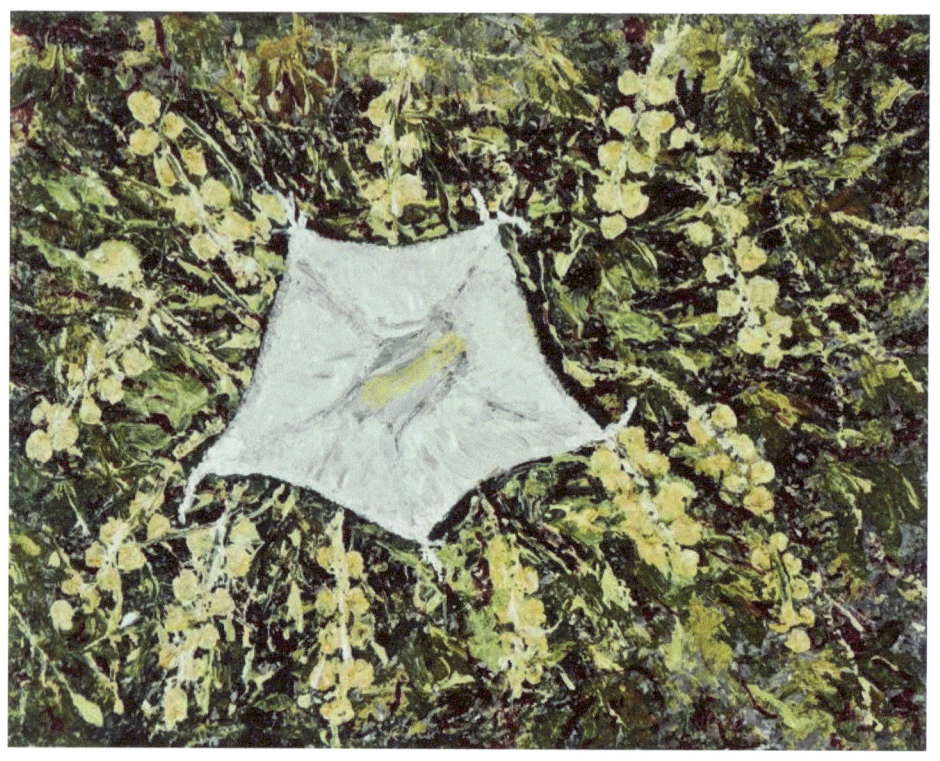

Acrylics on Canvas 16x20

Ernest & Laurel

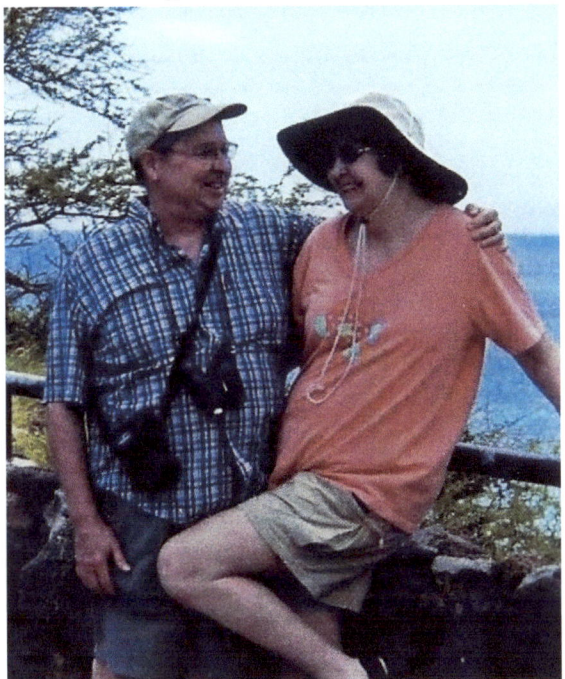

In Bermuda

LAUREL RICHARDSON is a Distinguished Emeritus Academy Professor of Sociology at The Ohio State University. She has been honored with Lifetime Achievement awards in her profession and in *Who's Who* in America and the world. Her most recent book is *Seven Minutes from home: An American Daughter's Story* (Sense: 2016). She has been married to the novelist and painter Ernest Lockridge for forty years. Most days she walks their two Papillons, writes, quilts, and walks the dogs some more.

ERNEST LOCKRIDGE received for his eighth birthday a set of Sargent Oil Paints in its brown and black cardboard box and wasting no time made his first painting that same day. Now, on the verge of his eightieth, following a career as novelist and Full Professor of English at The Ohio State University, where he was awarded "The O.S.U. Alumni Award for Distinguished Teaching"—his award-winning paintings appear in solo exhibits and on the covers of books, and in *Why I Love Ernest*, my most highly prized and deeply moving award ever.

www.ingramcontent.com/pod-product-compliance
Lightning Source LLC
Chambersburg PA
CBHW040324220526

45473CB00009B/2565